Easy-to-Make
Trend Jewelry

BOHEMIAN-INSPIRED DESIGNS
WITH TASSELS, STONES & CORD

DESIGN ORIGINALS
an Imprint of Fox Chapel Publishing
www.d-originals.com

We would like to acknowledge the extremely talented creative team at Cousin Corporation of America for their contributions to this book. A special thanks to Kristine Regan Daniel, Jennifer Eno-Wolf, and Chloe Pemberton for their additional support.

Acquisition editor: Peg Couch
Cover and page designers: Llara Pazdan & Justin Speers
Layout designer: Wendy Reynolds
Editors: Colleen Dorsey & Katie Weeber
Technical editor: Melissa Younger
Copy editor: Laura Taylor
Photography: Mike Mihalo
Photography styling: Llara Pazdan & Kati Erney

ISBN 978-1-4972-0312-9

© 2017 by Cousin Corporation of America and New Design Originals Corporation, *www.d-originals.com*, an imprint of Fox Chapel Publishing, 800-457-9112, 1970 Broad Street, East Petersburg, PA 17520.

Library of Congress Cataloging-in-Publication Control Number : 2017006733

Printed in the United States of America
First printing

You Can DIY This!

Jewelry making should be simple, right? Combine some natural cord with a collection of earthy beads, attach a clasp, and you're ready to go! But when you sit down to make a project, you might feel overwhelmed by all of the techniques and vocabulary. What is the difference between a seed bead and an E-bead, and how exactly do you tie a square knot? Don't be intimidated—this book is specifically designed to break it all down and keep things simple so you can unleash your creativity without fear. You'll build a foundation first, learning the basic vocabulary and techniques so you'll feel totally confident when you sit down to tackle your first project.

Diving into your first project means a trip to the craft store to gather your supplies. Shopping the jewelry aisle can be intimidating. There is always a vast array of options on display, and you don't want to arrive home to discover you missed an essential component. To keep your shopping trips straightforward and simple, each project includes a shopping list you can take to the store with you. Throw this book in your bag, or use your phone to snap a photo of the list so you are never in doubt about what you need.

Once you've made a few projects, you might get the DIY itch to make a few tweaks. And you should! That's the point of making your own jewelry, right? Instructions are provided for each project so you can reproduce the design exactly as you see it, but you should never hesitate to get creative and change it up. Each of us has a unique style, favorite color palette, and favorite outfit. If a design uses suede cord and you prefer ribbon, don't be afraid to make it with ribbon! The same goes for bead color and shape. If you see something cool in the beading aisle that you'd like to try, go for it!

This book sets you up with all of the tools you'll need to master DIY jewelry making. With a touch of your unique style and creativity, you can make these projects your own. It's time to dive in and get started!

Happy crafting!

Contents

Silver Forest Necklace

Suede & Chain Braided
Bracelet

Bright Boho Fringe
Earrings

Elephant Choker

Beaded Tassel Bangles

Boho Traveler
Earring Set

Beaded Suede Cord
Bracelet

Medallion Tassel
Necklace

Chunky Rope
Necklace

Chunky Rope
Bracelet

Beaded Purse Tassel

Deco Fringe
Earrings

Natural Knotted
Bracelet

Autumn Tassel
Necklace

Suede & Shell Cuff

Filigree Crystal
Earrings

Silver Shine Wrap
Choker

Gold Glimmer
Necklace

Green Goddess
Headpiece

Boho Stone Drop
Necklace

Getting Started

If you are totally new to jewelry making, this is the place to start.
This section will help you build a foundation by allowing you to familiarize
yourself with the common tools and materials used in jewelry making.
You'll also find step-by-step tutorials for the techniques you'll need to assemble
the projects in this book. When you're finished, you'll be able to spot nugget
beads when shopping at the craft store and be able to finish the ends of leather
cord and cotton rope with ease. Once you have a grasp of the content in
this section, you'll be ready to tackle your first jewelry project!

Tools

You don't need to spend a lot of money purchasing a vast array of tools to get started with jewelry making. A few sets of pliers and a handful of extras will allow you to make all of the projects in this book. Here are the common tools of jewelry making.

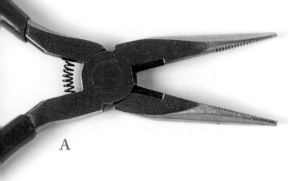

A

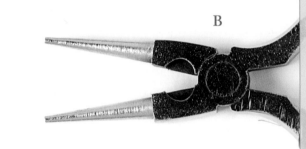

B

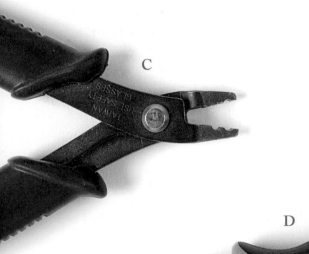

C

D

THE ESSENTIALS

Needle-nose pliers (A) come to a tapered point, making them the perfect tool to get into small areas of a jewelry design. Use this tool to hold small pieces, open and close jump rings, and manipulate wire.

Round-nose pliers (B) have rounded prongs that are used for making loops in wire, head pins, or eye pins.

Crimping pliers (C) are pliers made specifically for use with crimp tubes. The specially shaped grooves in these pliers will attach a crimp tube to beading wire in the most secure way possible.

Wire cutters (D) should always be used to cut jewelry wire—do not use scissors. Regular wire cutters that you get from the hardware store will work, but flush cutters made specifically for jewelry making are recommended.

THE EXTRAS

Memory wire cutters are heavy-duty wire cutters made specifically to cut the coils of memory wire without affecting their shape.

E-6000® glue is an extra-strong craft glue. It is perfect for securing cord ends or connecting other components.

A *jewelry hammer* is a lightweight hammer used for shaping metal. This hammer has two heads—a flat head and a round head.

A *ring mandrel* is a tapered rod used to measure the size of a ring or, in the case of jewelry making, to shape a ring to a specific size.

Beading tweezers are helpful when it comes to sorting and handling beads. Their extra-fine tip means they can pick up tiny beads more easily than your fingers can. Some tweezers come with a small, spoon-like scoop on the back end for easily collecting loose beads.

A *bead reamer* is like a mini drill that comes with an assortment of tips, which are used like drill bits. The tips can clean up the edges of a hole drilled in a bead, straighten the hole, or otherwise enlarge or re-shape the hole.

Awls are sharp, pointed tools used for making holes in leather.

TOOLS & MATERIALS

Beads

Of course beads are needed for jewelry making, but you might be surprised by the vast number of shapes and sizes that are available. What is the difference between a rondelle and a briolette? Take a look at this collection of commonly used beads to learn some important terms.

Seed beads (A) are extra-small beads, ranging in size from about 1.5mm to 3mm. Their sizes are listed as a number over zero (15/0, 12/0, etc.). The smaller the initial number, the larger the bead.

E-beads (B) are large seed beads, size 6/0, or about 4mm.

Bugle beads (C) are small, tube-shaped beads.

Cones (D) have a cone shape with a wide base at one end and a tapered point at the other. They are hollow, so they can fit over small components in a design.

Bicones (E) look like two cones that have been joined at the bottom. In profile, they have a diamond shape, with the widest point across the center and a tapered point at each end.

Rondelles (F) look like round, spherical beads that have been squashed just slightly. They look a bit like inner tubes.

Briolettes (G) have a teardrop or pear shape. They are almost always faceted (cut to have multiple faces, like a diamond) and always side-drilled, with a hole through the tapered point of the bead, rather than through the center of the bead.

Melon beads (H) actually have a pumpkin-like appearance, with raised, rounded sections running from top to bottom.

Beehive beads (I) are shaped like beehives you might see in cartoons with raised, rounded sections like rings running around the circumference of the bead.

Nuggets (J) have no specific shape. They are like pebbles you might pick up on the beach—random and unique.

Spacer beads (K) refer to small, plain, typically metallic beads. These beads serve an important function by adding space to a jewelry design without detracting from the focal beads.

Stringing Materials

Stringing materials include all of the items you can string beads onto or attach beads to. Stringing materials like cotton rope or hemp cord can also be used without beads to create jewelry using decorative knotwork. Here is a collection of common stringing materials.

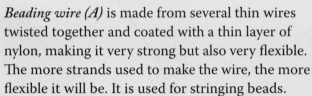

Beading wire (A) is made from several thin wires twisted together and coated with a thin layer of nylon, making it very strong but also very flexible. The more strands used to make the wire, the more flexible it will be. It is used for stringing beads.

Gauge wire (B) is a single piece of metal measured by the thickness of its diameter (gauge). The smaller the gauge number, the thicker the wire is. Gauge wire has varying flexibility and can be used for stringing beads, wire wrapping, or creating fixed components in a design.

Memory wire (C) is gauge wire that has been shaped into coils. The coils can be cut or stretched, but cannot be used for wrapping or other decorative wire work.

Cord (D) generally encompasses any non-wire material used for stringing beads. It is typically made of fabric, fiber, or natural materials. Cording includes satin, leather or suede, rope, or hemp.

Monofilament (E) is an often transparent synthetic cord, similar to fishing line. It is available in different strengths based on the amount of weight it can hold (2 lb. monofilament can hold two pounds of beads).

Chain (F) is a series of metal links joined together. The links may be closed (solid pieces of metal) or open (with a slit cut through them so they can be opened and removed from the main chain). Chain is available in a variety of shapes—cable, curb, and flat-link are the types you'll encounter the most in this book. (For more about different kinds of chain, see the glossary.)

Findings

Findings are all of the components used to build a piece of jewelry. They attach, link, and hold together all of the elements in a design. Here is a collection of common jewelry findings.

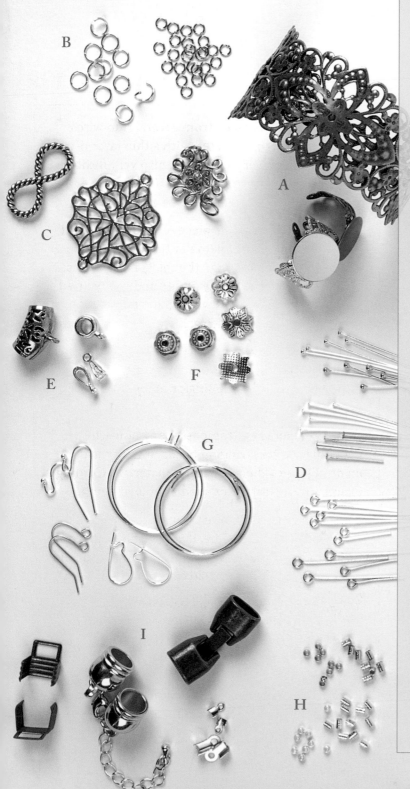

Bases (A) are unembellished blanks that you build upon to create a jewelry piece, such as a ring blank or a bangle bracelet blank.

Jump rings (B) are the most commonly used component to connect different pieces in a jewelry design. They are almost always "open" with a slit cut into the ring so it can be opened and closed. They are also available as solid rings, called closed jump rings.

Connectors (C) are bars, beads, or other components that have a loop (or loops) on each end. They are used to connect separate elements in a design.

Head pins, *ball head pins*, and *eye pins (D)* are short lengths of wire finished at one end with a flat head (head pin), ball (ball head pin), or loop (eye pin). Beads are strung onto the pins and the ends are formed into loops to create decorative bead drops or links.

Bails (E) are used to attach pendants to chain, cord, wire, or other stringing materials.

Bead caps (F) are bowl-shaped decorative components paired with beads. Their shape allows them to fit snugly against the bead as if they were part of it rather than a separate element.

Earring wires (G) encompass any component used to hook an earring to the ear. They come in a variety of shapes including hooks (also known as earring wires or French hooks), kidney wires, and hoops.

Crimp tubes and *crimp beads (H)* are used to finish the ends of beading wire.

Cord ends (I) are used to finish the ends of cord designs without knots. They come as caps that slide over the cord ends and are secured with glue, or crimps, which are clamped onto the cord ends.

Clasps (J, at top) are placed at the ends of a design and are used to close it. They come in numerous shapes and sizes including lobster clasps, toggle sets, or magnetic clasps.

Opening and Closing Jump Rings

Jump rings are used to connect different jewelry components to one another. Opening and closing a jump ring incorrectly can affect its shape or leave gaps that might allow jewelry components to fall off, so it's important to know how to do it properly.

Project(s) using this technique appear on pages 28, 30, 34, 36, 38, 40, 42, 44, 50, 54, 56, 58, 60, and 62.

1 *Position the pliers.* It is best to use two needle-nose pliers for this process. Using the pliers, grasp the ring on each side of the opening.

2 *Start twisting the ring open.* To keep the ring's shape, it should be twisted open, with the ends moving back to front instead of side to side. To do this, twist one wrist toward your body and the other wrist away from your body.

3 *Finish opening the ring.* Continue twisting until the opening is wide enough to attach the desired components. String on components like chain, clasps, or bead drops.

4 *Close the ring.* Following the method in Steps 1–3, reposition the pliers and twist the ring closed. If there is a gap, gently wiggle the pliers, moving the ends of the ring backward and forward while gently pressing them together. The ends should slightly overlap and then snap together tightly so the tension of the metal will hold the ring closed.

1

2

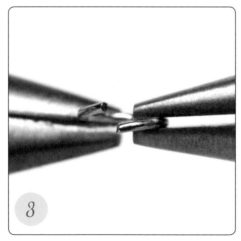

3

4

Split rings are like miniature key rings. They are made of coiled wire and do not have openings like jump rings, making them a more secure and sturdy option for heavy components. To attach items to a split ring, use a head pin or eye pin to hold the coils open.

Attaching Crimp Tubes/Beads

Crimp tubes and beads are used with beading wire and secured using crimping pliers. Once crimped, the tubes/beads stay in place on the wire, so they can be used to attach clasps or hold individual beads or groups of beads in a certain place.

Project(s) using this technique appear on pages 50 and 56.

1 *String the clasp.* String a crimp tube and a clasp (such as one half of a toggle clasp or a single lobster clasp) onto a strand of beading wire. Bring the end of the wire back through the crimp tube, creating a ½" (1.3cm) tail. Push the crimp tube up the wire so it is close to the clasp.

2 *Make the first crimp.* Place the crimp tube in the U-shaped groove of the crimping pliers (closest to the handles). Separate the wires in the crimp tube so they are parallel and do not cross. Firmly collapse the crimp tube, forming it into a U shape with one wire in each groove.

3 *Make the second crimp.* Place the crimp tube in the oval-shaped groove of the crimping pliers (farthest from the handles). Position the crimp tube so the U shape is sideways. Squeeze the pliers so the ends of the U shape come together.

4 *Check the wire.* Once crimped, the tube will look like this. Tug on the wire to be sure it is secure. The tail of the wire can be hidden in beads strung onto the wire.

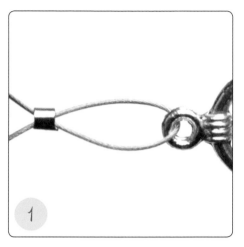

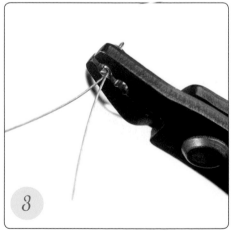

Crimp beads (below right) can be shaped using the crimp tube method described above. They are formed into smooth cylinders using the oval-shaped groove of the crimping pliers, or simply flattened using needle-nose pliers.

Attaching Crimped Cord Ends

Cord ends, crimped cord ends, and ribbon clamps are used to cleanly finish designs made with lengths of cord and ribbon. All cord ends and ribbon clamps have a loop attached to them that can be used to connect clasps or other components. For non-crimped cord ends, which are shaped similarly to bead caps or cones, you simply glue your cords into the cord end. But there is a specific technique for using crimped cord ends.

Project(s) using this technique appear on pages 36, 38, 56, and 62.

1 *Insert the cord.* If the design uses several cords, trim the ends flush and gather them together. Place the cord in the crimped cord end beneath the center plate.

2 *Fold down the center plate.* Use pliers to close the center plate, pinching the cord in place between the plate and the back of the crimped cord end.

3 *Fold down the sides.* Use pliers to fold down one side of the crimped cord end and then the other, applying firm and even pressure.

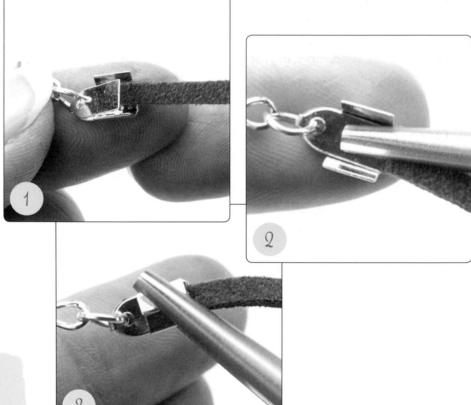

Place a dab of E-6000® glue inside the crimped cord end or ribbon clamp to help secure the cord or ribbon. This is particularly helpful if your design uses slippery satin cord or ribbon.

For ribbon clamps, simply gather the trimmed ends of the ribbons together in the clamp, squeeze the clamp closed with your fingers, and then use pliers to firmly close the clamp around the ribbons.

Cutting Chain

Jewelry projects often require lengths of chain that are shorter than what you can purchase. Use wire cutters to cut closed-link chain to the length needed. This method allows you to easily cut multiple pieces of chain to the same length without measuring each piece.

Project(s) using this technique appear on pages 24, 28, 44, 46, 50, 54, 56, 58, and 60.

1 ***Cut the first length.*** Measure the length of chain needed and use wire cutters to cut it off the original chain. Remember, the cut link will fall off, so do not include this in the measurement.

2 ***Cut the remaining lengths.*** Thread a head pin through an end link of the cut chain, then through an end link of the original chain. Line up the chain links, and cut the next length of chain to match the first. Repeat to cut the remaining pieces needed.

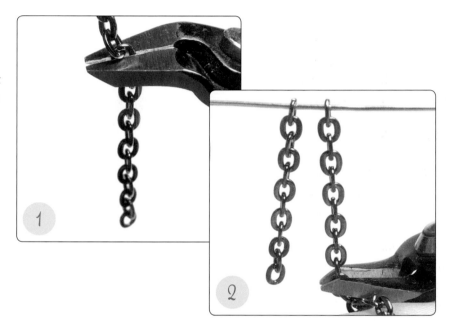

Open-Link Chain

Open chain links can be opened and closed just like jump rings (see page 12). Instead of cutting open-link chain, you can open and close the links to separate the necessary lengths of chain.

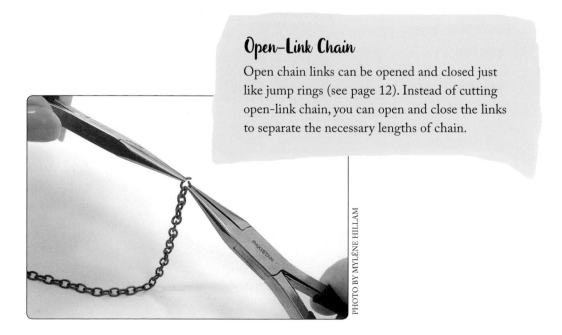

PHOTO BY MYLÈNE HILLAM

Forming a Loop

Round-nose pliers can be used to make loops in head pins, eye pins, or beading wire. Loops allow the pin or wire to be attached to other items using jump rings or other loops. Here's how to make a loop in an eye pin to create a bead link.

> Project(s) using this technique appear on pages 24, 30, 32, 34, 44, 46, 48, 50, 58, and 60.

1 **Trim the pin.** Slide a bead (or beads) onto an eye pin. Using needle-nose pliers, bend the tail of the eye pin to form a right angle with the bead(s). Trim the tail about ¼" (0.5cm) beyond the last bead.

2 **Start forming the loop.** Grasp the end of the wire with round-nose pliers. Rotate your wrist to wrap the wire around the pliers, forming a loop. The jaws of the pliers taper, so the size of the loop can be adjusted based on its position in the pliers.

3 **Finish forming the loop.** You may need to release the pin, reposition the pliers, and rotate them again to completely close the loop.

4 **Check the finished link.** When finished, there will be a loop on each side of the bead so other components can be attached to each side.

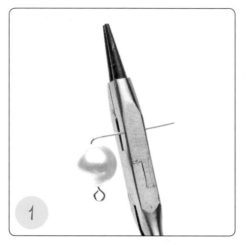

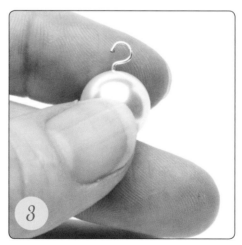

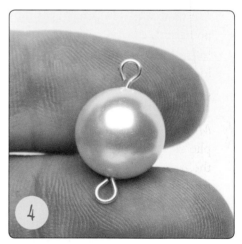

Tip: If you have trouble forming a loop at the end of a 1" (2.5cm) eye pin or head pin, you can always use a 2" (5cm) pin instead and simply trim off the excess.

Tip: You can convert a head pin to an eye pin by trimming off the flat head and forming a loop on that end instead.

Forming a Wrapped Loop

A wrapped loop is stronger than a basic loop, making it perfect for connecting heavy jewelry components. It also adds a decorative touch.

Project(s) using this technique appear on pages 36, 54, and 62.

1 *Bend the pin.* Slide a bead (or beads) onto a head pin. Grasp the head pin with round-nose pliers, resting the pliers against the top of the bead. Bend the tail of the pin to form a right angle with the bead(s).

2 *Start forming the loop.* Reposition the pliers so one prong is below the bend in the wire and one prong is above it. Wrap the tail of the head pin around the top prong, forming a loop.

3 *Finish forming the loop.* Reposition the pliers so the bottom prong is in the loop formed in Step 2. Finish forming the loop by wrapping the tail of the head pin around the bottom prong.

4 *Make the wrap.* Holding the loop with the pliers, wrap the tail of the head pin around the stem of the loop from the bottom of the loop to the top of the bead(s). Once the wrap is complete, trim away any excess from the tail of the head pin.

5 *Secure the tail.* Use needle-nose pliers or crimping pliers to tuck the trimmed tail into the wrap.

Tip: This technique works best with thin or soft metal that is pliable, like sterling.

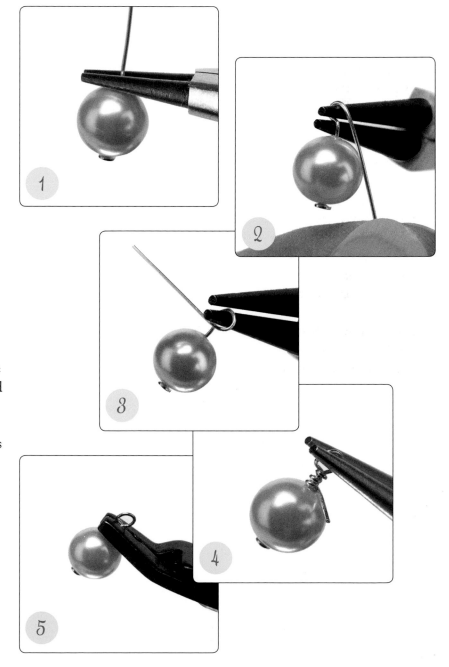

Forming a Loop for Briolette Beads

Briolettes and other side-drilled beads require a slightly different technique for creating a loop at the top of the bead. Adding a loop gives these types of beads the appearance of a pendant or bead drop.

Project(s) using this technique appear on page 58.

1 **Make the stem.** Grasp an eye pin directly under the loop with round-nose pliers. Partially bend the tail of the pin to the side at about a 45-degree angle, below the prong of the pliers, to form a short stem under the loop.

2 **Position the pin.** With the bead flat on a surface, set the loop and stem directly above the top of the bead with the bent tail off to one side of the bead. Use the pliers to slightly mark the spot on the tail of the pin where the pin will need to bend to go into the bead hole.

3 **Make the first bend.** Thread the tail of the pin through the bead up to the spot marked in Step 2. Then bend the wire flush up against the bead to reposition the loop and stem at the top of the bead. Press the pin against the bead to shape it to the curve of the bead, using round-nose pliers to help shape it as needed.

4 **Make the second bend.** Bend the other end of the pin flush up against the other side of the bead to mirror your first bend, smoothing the pin against the side of the bead.

5 **Make the wrap.** Wrap the tail of the pin around the stem from the top of the bead to the bottom of the loop. Trim away any excess from the tail of the pin, and use needle-nose pliers or crimping pliers to tuck the tail into the wrap.

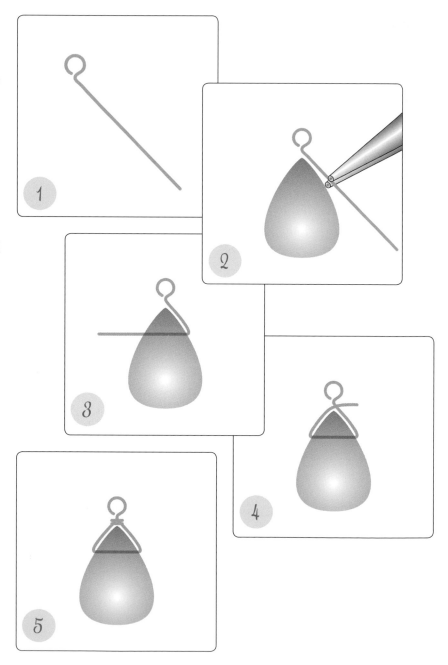

Forming Wire Wraps with Beads

With this technique, you can use wire to wrap beads securely around any charm or finding. Simply thread beads on as you go, following the instructions below.

Project(s) using this technique appear on pages 36 and 52.

1 *Attach the wire.* Cut a length of wire long enough to complete the desired wrap. Secure one end of the wire to the base component by wrapping it around the base three times.

2 *Add the first bead.* String a bead onto the wire, positioning the bead against the base. On the other side of the bead, wrap the wire around the base component twice to secure the bead in place. Then slide on another bead.

3 *Finish.* Repeat Step 2 until the desired number of beads has been added. Finish by wrapping the wire around the base component three times. Trim away any excess wire and use pliers to flatten the wire tail and loops snugly against the base.

Simple Knots

These basic knots are useful for starting and finishing designs, as well as attaching components.

Project(s) using this technique appear on pages 36, 38, 44, 48, 50, 56, and 62.

DOUBLE KNOT

This basic knot is the best knot to use for finishing designs made with elastic or stretch cord. It's the same knot you use to start tying your shoes—you just tie it twice! Before and after tying each knot, pull on the cord ends to stretch the elastic tight. For extra security, add a dot of clear nail polish or craft glue to the knot. Trim away any excess cord.

OVERHAND KNOT

Overhand knots can be used to start or finish a design, to hold components in place in a design, or to function as decorative elements. To tie an overhand knot with a loop, fold the cord in half to form a loop at the center. Then tie the knot as usual, positioning the loop so it extends out of the knot.

LARK'S HEAD KNOT

This knot is perfect for attaching cord to other objects, like a ring or pendant. Fold the cord in half to form a loop at the center. Pass the loop through the jewelry component (like the hole of a pendant) from front to back. Then, bring the ends of the cord through the loop and pull them to make the knot snug.

Double Knot

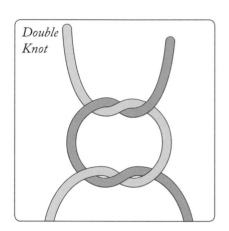

Overhand Knot

Lark's Head Knot

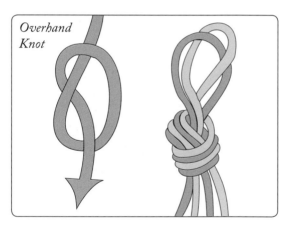

Square Knot

This decorative knot is commonly used in macramé and works well with hemp, rope, and other natural cording. For an embellished design, beads and other decorative components can be added to the cord as the knot is tied.

Project(s) using this technique appear on page 48.

1 **Prepare the cords.** Tie four cords together. If desired, secure the end of the cords in the clip of a clipboard or in a binder clip. Place the four cords side by side. The two outer cords (red) are the working cords, and the two center cords (purple) are the filler cords.

2 **Tie the knot.** For the first half of the knot, bring the left working cord over the filler cords and under the right working cord. Bring the right working cord under the center cords and over the left working cord. Pull tight. For the second half of the knot, bring the left working cord under the filler cords and over the right working cord. Bring the right working cord over the center cords and under the left working cord. Pull tight.

3 **Repeat.** Repeat Step 2 to the desired length.

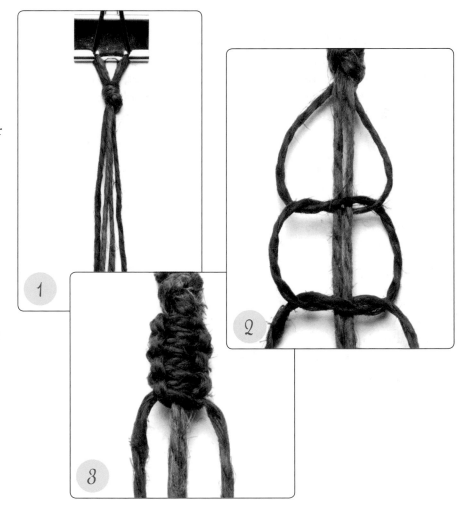

Adding Beads
Beads can be strung on the two filler cords or on either of the working cords.

Step-by-Step Projects

Now that you know the lingo and understand the basic techniques, it's time to put what you've learned into practice and make some projects. Remember to use the shopping lists to help navigate the jewelry section at the store. And don't be afraid to choose cord, beads, and colors that suit your personal taste to make a project your own!

Level:

Time:

The "Level" for each project indicates whether it is Beginner, Intermediate, or Advanced.

The "Time" for each project indicates how long each project will take, not including glue drying time. One diamond means less than an hour; two diamonds means between one and two hours; and three diamonds means more than two hours.

Silver Forest Necklace

This long pendant necklace includes leaf connectors and an owl charm for a fun hippie vibe. The classic style is appropriate year round, but it will be a perfect fit for any summer outfit. Try it with a long, flowing maxi dress.

1 *Make the bead links.* Slide 3 bicones onto an eye pin and form a loop. Repeat to make a total of 12 bead links.

2 *Prepare the chains.* Cut six 3¼" (8.5cm) lengths of chain.

3 *Connect the pieces.* Connect the following, in order: bead link, chain, bead link, leaf connector. Repeat until you have used all 12 bead links, 6 lengths of chain, and 5 leaf connectors to create the necklace chain. Make sure the leaf connectors are all facing the same direction.

4 *Add the pendant.* Connect the bead links at both ends of the necklace chain to the top loop of the owl pendant.

SHOPPING LIST

- 1 - Owl pendant with chain tassel (silver/teal)
- 36 - 4mm glass bicone beads (AB mirror blue/green)
- 5 - 1" (2.5cm) leaf connectors (silver)
- 22" (60cm) - 8mm rope chain (silver)
- 12 - 1" (2.5cm) eye pins (silver)

TOOLS

- Needle-nose pliers
- Round-nose pliers
- Wire cutters

TECHNIQUES

- Cutting Chain
- Forming a Loop

Suede & Chain Braided Bracelet

It doesn't get any easier than this project. The simple braided design makes this the perfect everyday piece to pair with any outfit. The chain incorporated in the braid adds a special touch to this streamlined design.

1 *Cut the cords.* Cut two lengths of cord to the desired wrist size, being sure to allow for the length of the cord ends.

2 *Join the cords.* Lay the two lengths of cord side by side. Place a very short piece of tape around each end of the joined cords to prevent unraveling.

3 *Add the cord ends.* Place glue into the opening of each cord end, push the ends of the cords in, and allow to dry thoroughly. It may be necessary to peel off the tape before gluing.

SHOPPING LIST

- 20" (51cm) - 10mm suede and chain braided cord (brown/silver)
- 1 - 34.75 x 13.5mm hook and loop cord end set (silver)

TOOLS

- Scissors
- Tape
- E-6000® glue

Bright Boho Fringe Earrings

Level:
♦ ● ●

Time:
♦ ● ●

These earrings are a rainbow of fun and a great way to add a pop of color to an outfit. This flirty look is perfect for summer. Pair them with a tank top or t-shirt and flip-flops. Switch up the pattern or the colors of the chain pieces to suit your style.

1 *Prepare the chains.* Cut the following lengths of chain: eight 1¼" (3.2cm) of purple/gold, eight 1¼" (3.2cm) of pink/gold, four 1¼" (3.2cm) of green/gold, and two 1⅜" (3.5cm) of blue/gold. Gather pairs of the same color together onto single jump rings so that you have 4 purple sets, 4 pink sets, 2 green sets, and 1 blue set.

2 *Add the blue set.* Connect the blue set to the bottom middle loop of a half-circle connector.

3 *Add the green sets.* Connect the 2 green sets to the next loop to the left and right of the blue set.

4 *Add the pink sets.* Connect the 4 pink sets to the next 2 loops to the left and right of the green sets.

5 *Add the purple sets.* Connect the 4 purple sets to the next 2 loops to the left and right of the pink sets.

6 *Prepare the final chains.* Cut two 1¼" (3.2cm) lengths of purple/gold chain. Use 4mm jump rings to connect one end of each length of chain to the top side of the end loops on each side of the half-circle connector.

7 *Add the earring wire.* Use one 4mm jump ring to connect the other end of both purple/gold chains from Step 6 to an earring wire.

8 *Make the other earring.* Repeat Steps 1–7 for the matching earring.

SHOPPING LIST

- 2 - 15 x 32mm half-circle connectors (antique gold/rhinestone)
- 36" (92cm) - 1.8mm flat-link cable chain (purple/gold)
- 26" (66cm) - 1.8mm flat-link cable chain (pink/gold)
- 14" (36cm) - 1.8mm flat-link cable chain (green/gold)
- 8" (21cm) - 1.8mm flat-link cable chain (blue/gold)
- 28 - 4mm jump rings (antique gold)
- 2 - Earring wires (antique gold)

TOOLS

- Needle-nose pliers
- Wire cutters

TECHNIQUES

- Opening and Closing Jump Rings
- Cutting Chain

Elephant Choker

This choker uses a simple design for bold impact. Adjust the length of the leather cord to get the exact style you want. Play up the tribal style of this piece by pairing it with a bold animal print.

1 *Make the clasp.* Use a 6mm jump ring to connect the lobster clasp to one cord end. Use another 6mm jump ring to connect the extender chain to the other cord end.

2 *Make the necklace base.* Cut the leather cord to the desired neck length, allowing for the length of the cord ends and lobster clasp. If necessary, trim the ends of the cord to fit into the cord ends. Place a dab of glue into each cord end, insert the ends of the cord, and allow to dry.

3 *Add a jump ring.* Use a bead reamer or small point awl to punch a small hole through the middle front of the leather cord. Attach a 6mm jump ring through the hole.

4 *Add the bead link.* Slide a black bicone onto an eye pin and form a loop to make a bead link. Use a 4mm jump ring to attach one end of the bead link to the 6mm jump ring from Step 3 so that the bead link hangs down in the middle of the choker.

5 *Add the charm.* Connect the elephant charm to the loop on the bottom of the bead link.

SHOPPING LIST

- 1 - Elephant charm (antique gold)
- 1 - 6mm crystal bicone bead (black)
- 13–16" (33–41cm) - ⅜" (1cm) decorative flat leather cord (gold/black)
- 2 - 10mm cord ends for flat leather (gold)
- 1 - 2" (5cm) extender chain (gold)
- 1 - 1" (2.5cm) eye pin (antique gold)
- 3 - 6mm jump rings (antique gold)
- 1 - 4mm jump ring (antique gold)
- 1 - Lobster clasp (gold)

TOOLS

- Needle-nose pliers
- Wire cutters
- Scissors
- Craft glue
- Bead reamer or small point awl

TECHNIQUES

- Opening and Closing Jump Rings
- Forming a Loop

Beaded Tassel Bangles

The bold neon color of these bangles screams summer, and the tassels add an additional element of fun. Pair these with other bright colors for a youthful, modern look. Or, for a bold effect, wear them with an all-black outfit so the color really pops. If you love the tassel look, add more!

1   *Prepare the wire.* Cut 3 separate rings of the memory wire, so the ends just slightly overlap. Form a loop on one end of each ring.

2   *Make two simple bangles.* String 23 yellow beads onto one ring. Form a loop on the other end to finish the bangle. Repeat to make a second identical beaded bangle.

3   *Make the tassel bangle.* On the third ring, string on 4 yellow beads, 1 tassel, 5 yellow beads, 1 tassel, 5 yellow beads, 1 tassel, 5 yellow beads, 1 tassel, and 4 yellow beads. Form a loop on the other end to finish the bangle.

 SHOPPING LIST

- 69 - 8mm round beads (matte neon yellow)
- 4 - Tassels with jump rings attached (neon yellow)
- 3+ - Coils memory wire, 2½" (6.4cm) diameter

TOOLS

- Round-nose pliers
- Memory wire cutters

TECHNIQUES

- Forming a Loop

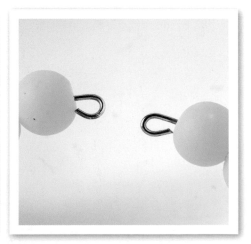

Boho Traveler Earring Set

If you have a bit of wanderlust, you will appreciate the Eastern vibe of these earrings. To enhance the style, pair them with a tunic top or a printed dress in bold colors. Have fun shopping for connectors and charms that capture your love of travel.

LIGHT BLUE ELEPHANT EARRINGS

1 *Create the bead links.* Slide a 6mm light blue bicone, a 4mm light blue bicone, and 5 light blue seed beads onto an eye pin and form a loop to make a bead link. Repeat to make a second bead link.

2 *Finish the earrings.* Connect the seed bead end of a bead link to the loop of an antique gold earring wire and the other end of the bead link to a large elephant charm. Repeat with the remaining bead link to make the matching earring.

ELEPHANT/HAMSA HAND EARRINGS

1 *Create the bead links.* Slide a red glass round bead onto an eye pin and form a loop to make a bead link. Connect one end of the bead link to a small elephant charm. Repeat to make a second bead link and connect it to the remaining small elephant charm.

2 *Finish the earrings.* Use a 6mm antique gold jump ring to connect the other end of a bead link from Step 1 to the bottom of a hamsa hand charm. Connect the top of the hamsa hand charm to an antique gold earring wire. Repeat to make the matching earring.

COPPER MANDALA EARRINGS

1 *Create the earrings.* Use a 4mm copper jump ring to connect a 22mm copper/turquoise/red filigree charm to one side of an 18mm copper/teal flower connector. Repeat with the remaining charm and connector.

2 *Attach the earring wires.* Connect the other side of one of the 18mm copper/teal flower connectors to a copper earing wire. Repeat to make the matching earring.

SHOPPING LIST

- 10 - 11/0 seed beads (light blue)
- 2 - 4mm crystal bicone beads (light blue)
- 2 - 6mm crystal bicone beads (light blue)
- 2 - 6mm glass round beads (red)
- 2 - Large elephant charms (antique gold/light blue)
- 2 - Small elephant charms (antique gold/red)
- 2 - Open hamsa hand charms (antique gold/blue)
- 2 - 22mm filigree charms (copper/turquoise/red)
- 2 - 17mm flower connectors (copper/teal)
- 4 - 2" (5cm) eye pins (antique gold)
- 2 - 6mm jump rings (antique gold)
- 2 - 4mm jump rings (copper)
- 4 - Earring wires (antique gold)
- 2 - Earring wires (copper)

TOOLS

- Needle-nose pliers
- Round-nose pliers
- Wire cutters

TECHNIQUES

- Opening and Closing Jump Rings
- Forming a Loop

Beaded Suede Cord Bracelet

Level:
◆ ● ●

Time:
◆ ● ●

The beaded wire wrap gives this simple bracelet a unique twist. Pair it with a peasant blouse and a large floppy hat. To change up the look, try colored cord or use opaque beads to highlight the center ring.

1 **Wrap the wire.** Wrap one end of the 20-gauge wire a few times around the circle link. Add two amethyst bicones and one smoke bicone to the wire. Wrap the wire with the bicones around the circle link so the bicones show on the top side of the link. Continue repeating this pattern until you have wrapped the entire circumference of the circle link, but make sure you have 1 amethyst bicone left. Wrap the wire a few times around the link to secure it and trim away the excess.

2 **Attach the bead drop.** Slide the last amethyst bicone onto a head pin. Form a wrapped loop to connect the bicone to the end link on one side of the extender chain.

3 **Make the cords.** Cut two 7½" (19cm) lengths of suede cord. Bring both ends of one cord together, side by side, and fold a crimped cord end around the ends to secure them. Repeat with the second cord.

4 **Attach and finish.** Use a lark's head knot to attach each cord to opposite sides of the circle link. Use a 4mm jump ring to connect one crimped cord end to a lobster clasp. Use another 4mm jump ring to connect the other crimped cord end to the extender chain.

SHOPPING LIST

- 21 - 4mm glass bicone beads (amethyst)
- 12 - 4mm glass bicone beads (smoke)
- 1 - 27mm circle link (antique gold)
- 24" (61cm) - 20-gauge wire (silver)
- 15" (38cm) - ⅛" (0.3cm)-wide suede cord (brown)
- 2 - 4mm crimped cord ends (antique gold)
- 1 - 2" (5cm) extender chain (antique gold)
- 1 - 1" (2.5cm) head pin (antique gold)
- 2 - 4mm jump rings (antique gold)
- 1 - Lobster clasp (antique gold)

TOOLS

- Needle-nose pliers
- Round-nose pliers
- Wire cutters
- Scissors

TECHNIQUES

- Opening and Closing Jump Rings
- Attaching Crimped Cord Ends
- Forming a Wrapped Loop
- Forming Wire Wraps with Beads
- Simple Knots: Lark's Head Knot

Level:
♦ ● ●

Time:
♥ ♥ ●

Medallion Tassel Necklace

The brown cord and floral pendant in this necklace give off an earthy boho vibe. Be sure to pack this for your next weekend away at a music festival. Pair it with an oversize t-shirt, jeans, and a pair of matching brown boots.

1 *Prepare the pendant.* Attach a 4mm jump ring to each of the pendant's holes. Attach the loop of a bail to the top jump ring.

2 *Make the tassel.* Cut one 4" (10cm) and ten 5" (13cm) lengths of cotton cord. Align all the 5" (13cm) cord ends evenly and thread them through a 6mm jump ring. Fold the cords in half on the jump ring. Wrap the 4" (10cm) cord around the folded cords near the top a few times and tie a double knot. Trim the excess cord from the knot and trim the tassels evenly. Attach the tassel jump ring to the 4mm jump ring at the bottom of the pendant.

3 *Braid the necklace.* Cut six 25" (64cm) lengths of cord. Gather the strands together at one end and attach a crimped cord end. Braid the 6 strands together in 3 sets of 2 strands. To do this, place 3 sets of 2 cords side by side. Bring the left set of cords over the center set of cords. Then, bring the right set of cords over the new center set of cords (see illustration A). Repeat, bringing the left set of cords over the center set of cords then the right set of cords over the center set of cords until the braid reaches the desired length (see illustration B).

SHOPPING LIST

- 1 - Metal pendant (gold/turquoise)
- 17' (520cm) - Cotton cord (brown)
- 2 - Crimped cord ends (gold)
- 1 - Bail (gold)
- 1 - 3" (7.5cm) extender chain (gold)
- 2 - 4mm jump rings (gold)
- 3 - 6mm jump rings (gold)
- 1 - Lobster clasp (gold)

TOOLS

- Needle-nose pliers
- Wire cutters

TECHNIQUES

- Opening and Closing Jump Rings
- Attaching Crimped Cord Ends
- Simple Knots: Double Knot

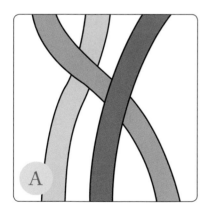

A

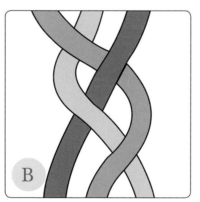

B

Tip: If your pendant only has one hole, use a small drill bit or a small punch and hammer to make a matching hole opposite the pre-drilled hole.

4 *Finish the necklace.* After the desired necklace length is reached, slide on the bail so that it sits in the middle of the necklace. Bring the 6 strands together, trim them, and attach another crimped cord end.

5 *Add the clasp.* Attach a lobster clasp to one cord end using a 6mm jump ring. Attach an extender chain to the other cord end using another 6mm jump ring.

Chunky Rope Necklace

This necklace, along with its companion bracelet on page 42, is super simple and will come together quickly. Have fun mixing and matching the frames and links to create a varied look.

Level: ♦ ● ●

Time: ♦ ● ●

*1 **Connect the ropes.** Cut three 20" (51cm) and three 26" (66cm) lengths of cotton rope cord. Hold one group of ropes parallel and fold it in half to form a loop at the center. Thread the second group of ropes through this loop. Fold the second group of ropes in half so the two groups of rope are even and connected by their center loops.*

*2 **String one side.** Hold the ends of the 26" (66cm) ropes together and string on about 3" (7.6cm) of a random combination of the various links, donuts, and frames.*

*3 **String the other side.** Hold the ends of the 20" (51cm) ropes together and string on about 1½" (3.8cm) of a random combination of the various links, donuts, and frames.*

*4 **Attach the clasp.** Use 8mm jump rings to connect a cord end to each half of the toggle clasp set.*

*5 **Attach the cord ends.** Place glue in one cord end. Push the loose 20" (51cm) rope ends into the cord end and allow the glue to dry. Repeat with the remaining cord end and the 26" (66cm) ropes.*

SHOPPING LIST

- 5 - 18mm square frames (gunmetal)
- 4 - 18mm square frames (copper)
- 5 - 18mm square frames (antique gold)
- 5 - 21mm smooth metal donuts (bronze)
- 4 - 21mm hammered metal donuts (bronze)
- 5 - 30mm large wood links (brown)
- 5 - 20mm chain links (antique gold)
- 8 - 24mm chain links (antique gold)
- 12' (365cm) - 7mm cotton rope cord (cream)
- 2 - 14 x 20mm cord ends (silver)
- 2 - 8mm jump rings (silver)
- 1 - Large toggle clasp set (silver)

TOOLS

- Needle-nose pliers
- Scissors
- Craft glue

TECHNIQUES

- Opening and Closing Jump Rings

Level:
♦ ♦ •

Time:
♦ • •

Chunky Rope Bracelet

This bracelet adds some extra knotting to the basic design of its companion necklace on page 40. The necklace and bracelet set will pair well with a casual summer outfit like a tank top, cropped pants, and wedges.

1 *Attach the clasp.* Use the 6mm jump ring to connect the lobster clasp to the silver cord end.

2 *Attach the rope.* Cut two 24" (61cm) lengths of rope cord. Holding the ropes parallel, fold them in half to form a loop at the center. Attach the ropes to the square copper frame using a lark's head knot.

3 *Make three groups of rings.* Divide the circle frames, donuts, and round chain links into 3 roughly equal mixed groups.

4 *Make the first section.* Lay the four rope strands out straight, side by side. Take the two center ropes, bring them over and around the outer ropes, then underneath the outer ropes and back up so they are once again in the center. Take one group of circle frames from Step 3 and string them onto the two center ropes.

5 *Make the remaining sections.* Repeat Step 4, wrapping the center ropes over and around the outer ropes and sliding on another set of circle frames. Repeat one last time to string on the final set of rings.

6 *Trim the ends.* Trim the rope ends evenly according to the desired length for the finished bracelet. Be sure to factor in the length of the large silver cord end (remember, the rope ends will be glued into the cord end) and the length of the lobster clasp.

7 *Attach the cord end.* Place glue in the silver cord end from Step 1. Push the loose rope ends into the cord end and allow the glue to dry.

SHOPPING LIST

- 6 - 10mm circle frames (copper)
- 5 - 10mm circle frames (gunmetal)
- 6 - 10mm donuts (bronze)
- 8 - 16mm round chain links (antique gold)
- 1 - 18mm square frame (copper)
- 48" (122cm) - 7mm cotton rope cord (cream)
- 1 - 14 x 20mm metal cord end (silver)
- 1 - 6mm jump ring (silver)
- 1 - 28 x 14mm lobster clasp (silver)

TOOLS

- Needle-nose pliers
- Scissors
- Craft glue

TECHNIQUES

- Opening and Closing Jump Rings

Beaded Purse Tassel

Show off your style with this fun and flirty purse tassel. It makes a wonderful accent for a bag or a zipper pull for a large clutch. Select a charm that expresses who you are. If you love this look, you don't have to limit yourself to just one. Make several tassels to mix and match!

1   *Start the tassel.* Cut a 12" (31cm) length of ramie cord and set it aside. Wrap the entire remaining length of cord around the cardboard square (across 2 sides only). Cut the loops of cord wrapped around the square on one side to create a bundle of about 30 tassel cords that are all roughly the same length (about 11" [28cm] long). Slide three 6mm jump rings onto the center of the 12" (31cm) cord. Then tie this 12" (31cm) cord around the center of the bundle of tassel cords with a double knot, keeping the jump rings at the center.

2   *Finish the tassel.* Fold the gathered tassel cords in half over the knotted part of the tying cord to hide the knot and to form the tassel shape with the jump rings sticking out from the top. About ½" (1.5cm) below the top of the tassel, wrap the two ends of the tying cord in opposite directions around the tassel cords. Secure the ends of the tying cord with another double knot and trim away any excess cord.

3   *Start the toggle clasp decoration.* Use a 6mm jump ring to attach the large charm to the circle half of a toggle clasp.

4   *Bead the double strands.* Cut a 12" (31cm) length of monofilament. Use a lark's head knot to attach the monofilament to the circle half of the toggle clasp. String about 3½" (9cm) of bicones (about 22 bicones) onto one side of the monofilament. Bring the end of the monofilament back up through the bottom bicone and tie the end onto the strand to secure it. Trim away any excess monofilament. Repeat with the other side of the monofilament so that you have 2 strands of beads coming from the single lark's head knot.

5   *Bead the single strand.* Repeat Step 4 to attach another strand of monofilament to the toggle clasp on the other side of the bird charm. This time, though, instead of stringing beads onto each strand of the monofilament separately, string the beads onto both strands of the monofilament at once, so that you have 1 strand of beads coming from the single lark's head knot.

6   *Make the chain decoration.* Cut a 1¾" (4.5cm) length of chain. Use a 4mm jump ring to connect the small charm to the one end of the chain. Slide 1 clear bicone onto a head pin and form a loop to make a bead drop. Repeat with the remaining 3 clear bicones and 2 purple bicones to make a total of 6 bead drops. Attach each bead drop to a single link of the chain, starting from the bottom link just above the jump ring

SHOPPING LIST

- 112 - 11/0 seed beads (gunmetal)
- 68 - 4mm glass bicone beads (AB mirror aqua/bronze)
- 4 - 8mm glass bicone beads (clear)
- 2 - 8mm glass bicone beads (purple)
- 1 - Large charm (silver filigree bird)
- 1 - Small charm (freedom tag)
- 32' (975cm) - Ramie cord (multicolored ombré)
- 48" (125cm) - 2 lb. monofilament (clear)
- 1¾" (4.5cm) - 1.8mm curb chain (silver)
- 6 - 1" (2.5cm) head pins (silver)
- 4 - 6mm jump rings (silver)
- 1 - 4mm jump ring (silver)
- 1 - Toggle clasp set (silver)
- 1 - Swivel carabiner snap hook (silver)

TOOLS

- Needle-nose pliers
- Round-nose pliers
- Wire cutters
- Scissors
- Craft glue
- 6" (15.5cm) cardboard square

TECHNIQUES

- Opening and Closing Jump Rings
- Cutting Chain
- Forming a Loop
- Simple Knots: Double Knot
- Simple Knots: Lark's Head Knot

attaching the small charm. Connect the other end of the chain to the 6mm jump ring from Step 3.

7 *Make the beaded loops.* Cut a 6" (15.5cm) length of monofilament. String on about 26–28 seed beads so that the strand will fit snugly around the top of the tassel when formed into a loop. Tie the ends of monofilament together into a secure knot to form a closed beaded loop. Trim away any excess cord. Repeat to make a total of 4 beaded loops.

8 *Add the beaded loops and decorated tassel.* Slide 1 of the beaded loops from Step 7 down around the top of the tassel, positioning it just below the tying cord. Slide the decorated toggle clasp down over the top of the tassel, positioning it to cover the tying cord. Slide the remaining 3 beaded loops onto the tassel above the decorated toggle clasp. For extra security, add a drop of craft glue underneath each of the items added to the tassel in this step.

9 *Add the carabiner.* Connect each of the 3 jump rings at the top of the tassel to the bottom of the carabiner hook.

Level:
♦♦♦

Time:
♦♦♦

Deco Fringe Earrings

These deco-style earrings have loads of personality. The bold turquoise connector and long chain fringe will make them the standout item of any outfit. Wear these on a fun night out, paired with matching turquoise pieces like a clutch or shoes.

1 *Make triple bead links.* Slide 3 rondelles onto an eye pin and form a loop to make a bead link. Repeat to make a total of 2 triple bead links.

2 *Make double bead links.* Slide 2 rondelles onto an eye pin and form a loop to make a bead link. Repeat to make a total of 2 double bead links.

3 *Make a single bead link.* Slide 1 rondelle onto an eye pin and form a loop to make a single bead link.

4 *Add the chains.* Cut fifteen 2" (5cm) lengths of chain. Connect one end of 3 lengths of chain to the loop on one end of each of the 5 bead links from Steps 1–3.

5 *Attach the links.* Attach the loop on the other end of each bead link to the bottom loops of a gold/turquoise connector as follows: the single bead link in the middle, double bead links to the left and right of the single bead link, and triple bead links to the left and right of the double bead links.

6 *Add the earring wire.* Attach an earring wire to the top loop of the gold/turquoise connector.

7 *Make the other earring.* Repeat Steps 1–6 for the matching earring.

SHOPPING LIST

- 22 - 4mm glass faceted rondelle beads (AB mirror gold/blue)
- 2 - 47 x 19mm deco five-loop connectors (gold/turquoise)
- 60" (155cm) - 1.8mm flat-link cable chain (black/gold)
- 10 - 1" (2.5cm) eye pins (antique gold)
- 2 - Earring wires (antique gold)

TOOLS

- Needle-nose pliers
- Round-nose pliers
- Wire cutters

TECHNIQUES

- Cutting Chain
- Forming a Loop

Natural Knotted Bracelet

Level:
💎 💎 •

Time:
💎 💎 •

This bracelet has a simple boho look that is elevated by the bead drop embellishments. The length and number of wraps can be adjusted to fit your wrist and your preference. The design's earthy look comes from the colors of the materials. Use all black cord with clear and silver beads for a simple, chic look or colorful cord and beads for a fun, vibrant look.

1. *Make the loop.* Hold the two lengths of hemp cord together and fold them in half to form a loop in the middle that is just large enough for the wood bead to fit through securely. Tie an overhand knot at the base of the loop. Place the loop underneath the clip on the clipboard so the cord ends hang down.

2. *Tie a set of tan knots.* Position the cords so the two silver cords are in the middle and the two tan cords are on each side. Just after the overhand knot, use the tan cords to tie three consecutive square knots around the silver cords.

3. *Tie a set of silver knots.* Bring the two tan cords over the silver cords so the tan cords are now in the middle. About ½" (1.3cm) beyond the last square knot, use silver cords to tie three consecutive square knots around the tan cords.

4. *Tie a set of tan knots.* Bring the silver cords over the tan cords so the silver cords are now in the middle. About ½" (1.3cm) beyond the last square knot, use tan cords to tie three consecutive square knots around the silver cords.

5. *Finish the knots.* Repeat Steps 3 and 4 about 10–12 more times so the bracelet will wrap around the wrist 3 times.

6. *Attach the bead.* Bring the ends of the two silver cords through the hole in the wooden bead. Bring all the cord ends together (with the tan cords outside of the bead) and tie a snug overhand knot. Trim the cord ends to the desired length.

7. *Make the bead drops.* Slide a single E-bead onto a head pin and form a loop to make a bead drop. Make a clear bead drop for every set of tan square knots in the bracelet and a gold bead drop for every set of silver square knots in the bracelet.

8. *Attach the bead drops.* Connect the loop of each clear bead drop to the middle square knot in each set of tan square knots and the loop of each gold bead drop to the middle square knot in each set of silver square knots.

SHOPPING LIST

- 1 - Large side-drilled wood bead (brown)
- 12–14 - 6/0 E-beads (clear)
- 12–14 - 6/0 E-beads (matte gold)
- 9' (275cm) - Hemp cord (silver twist)
- 9' (275cm) - Hemp cord (tan)
- 24–28 - 1" (2.5cm) head pins (antique gold)

TOOLS

- Needle-nose pliers
- Round-nose pliers
- Wire cutters
- Scissors
- Tweezers
- Clipboard

TECHNIQUES

- Forming a Loop
- Simple Knots: Overhand Knot
- Square Knot

Level:
◆◆●

Time:
◆●●

Autumn Tassel Necklace

You decide how you wear this necklace! The suede cords can be tied at the back or wrapped to create a choker look. To make the oranges in this design really pop, wear this piece with a turquoise top.

1 *Make the bead link.* Slide the orange crackle bead onto the eye pin and form a double loop to make a bead link. (Follow the instructions for forming a loop on page 16, but wrap the wire around the round-nose pliers twice to make it a double loop.)

2 *Make the chain tassel.* Cut twelve 2" (5cm) lengths of 2mm copper curb chain. Attach one end of each length of chain to a 6mm jump ring. Connect the jump ring to the bottom single loop of the bead link from Step 1 to make a chain tassel at the bottom of the bead link.

3 *Prepare the chain.* Cut two 3½" (9cm) lengths of 6mm copper curb chain. Connect a separate 6mm jump ring to both ends of both lengths of chain.

4 *Attach the beading wire.* Cut an 8" (20.5cm) length of beading wire. Use a crimp tube to connect one end of the wire to a 6mm jump ring on one of the 6mm chains from the Step 3.

5 *String the lower section.* String the following onto the beading wire: 6 orange/cream beads, 6 bronze bicones, the top double loop of the tasseled bead link from Step 2, 6 bronze bicones, and 6 orange/cream beads. Use a crimp tube to connect the other end of the beading wire to a 6mm jump ring on the other length of 6mm chain from Step 3.

6 *Prepare the beading wire.* Cut a 12" (30.5cm) length of beading wire. Use a crimp tube to connect one end of the beading wire to a new 6mm jump ring.

7 *String the upper section.* String a bronze bicone and an orange/cream bead onto the beading wire. Repeat this pattern 19 more times and finish with a bronze bicone. Use a crimp tube to connect the other end of the beading wire to a new 6mm jump ring.

8 *Connect the upper and lower sections.* Using the jump rings, connect one length of 6mm curb chain to one end of the upper beaded section from Step 7. Connect the other length of 6mm curb chain to the other end of the beaded section, so that the beaded section sits above the section with the tassel.

 SHOPPING LIST

- 1 - 24 x 20mm acrylic bead (orange crackle)
- 32 - 10mm glass rondelle beads (AB mirror orange/cream)
- 33 - 4mm glass bicone beads (metallic bronze/copper)
- 7½" (19cm) - 6mm curb chain (copper)
- 28" (72cm) - 2mm curb chain (copper)
- 70" (180cm) - 3mm suede cord (brown)
- 20" (51cm) - Beading wire (copper)
- 4 - Crimp tubes (copper)
- 1 - 2" (5cm) eye pin (copper)
- 7 - 6mm jump rings (copper)

TOOLS

- Needle-nose pliers
- Round-nose pliers
- Crimping pliers
- Wire cutters

TECHNIQUES

- Opening and Closing Jump Rings
- Attaching Crimp Tubes/Beads
- Cutting Chain
- Forming a Loop
- Simple Knots: Overhand Knot

9   *Attach the ties.* Cut two 35" (89cm) lengths of suede cord. Using an
overhand knot, tie the end of one cord to the 6mm jump ring at the end
of one of the 6mm curb chains that is connected to the beaded section
from Step 5. Tie an overhand knot in the other end of the suede cord.
Repeat to attach the other 35" (89cm) cord to the corresponding 6mm
jump ring on the other side of the necklace. Trim any excess cord after
testing the fit and deciding how the necklace will be worn.

Level:
◆◆●

Time:
◆◆●

Suede & Shell Cuff

This coastal piece should travel with you for any beach getaway weekend. Or use it to infuse your everyday style with a bit of sand and surf. This design will also look great with a darker suede, aqua chip beads, and gold wire.

1 *Cut the wire.* Cut thirteen 10"–20" (25–50cm) lengths of 28-gauge wire. The wire lengths will depend on the size of the beads in each cluster.

2 *Wrap the oval beads.* String an oval bead onto one length of wire and center the bead on the wire. Then, wrap each wire end several times around the bead as desired. Wrap the remaining free wire on each end around a bracelet strip several times to attach the wrapped bead to the bracelet. Trim away any excess wire. Repeat with the remaining oval beads. If desired, add a chip bead on top of an oval bead.

3 *Wrap the chip beads.* Group the chip beads into 8 groups of 1–5 beads as desired. Thread one length of wire through all the beads in one bead group and center the group on the wire. Wrap each end of the wire around a bracelet strip several times to attach the group to the bracelet. If desired, wrap the wire across the top of the group too, similar to how the oval beads were wrapped. Trim away any excess wire. Repeat with the remaining bead groups.

SHOPPING LIST

- 5 - 16 x 20mm flat oval shell beads (white)
- 24–30 - Shell chip beads (peach)
- 11'–22' (335–670cm) - 28-gauge wire (silver)
- 1 - 8" (20cm) suede bangle bracelet with strips and snap closures (tan)

TOOLS

- Wire cutters

TECHNIQUES

- Forming Wire Wraps with Beads

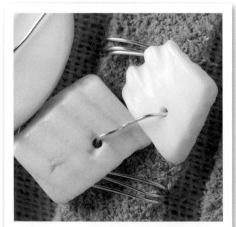

Filigree Crystal Earrings

Level:
♦ ♦ ●

Time:
♦ ● ●

The chain bead drops give the classic silhouette of these earrings an updated twist. The understated look will make the transition from day to evening a breeze. At work, pair these with other simple silver pieces. For a night out, punch up the look with rhinestone accessories.

1 **Cut the chains.** Cut the following lengths of chain: 1½" (3.8cm), 1¼" (3.2cm), and 1" (2.6cm).

2 **Gather the chains.** Attach one end of each of the 3 lengths of chain to a single jump ring.

3 **Connect the pieces.** Use the jump ring from Step 2 to connect the bottom loop of an earring wire to the top loop of a filigree pendant so the chains hang down behind the pendant.

4 **Make the bead drops.** Slide a spacer bead and a bicone onto a head pin and form a wrapped loop connecting the bead drop to the bottom link in one of the chains. Repeat 2 more times to attach a bead drop to each of the other 2 lengths of chain.

5 **Make the other earring.** Repeat Steps 1–4 for the matching earring.

 SHOPPING LIST

- 6 - 4mm crystal bicone beads (clear)
- 6 - 3.4mm daisy spacer beads (silver)
- 2 - 24mm filigree pendants (silver/ rhinestone)
- 10" (26cm) - 1.8mm cable chain (silver)
- 6 - 1" (2.5cm) head pins (silver)
- 2 - 4mm jump rings (silver)
- 2 - Flower earring wires (silver)

TOOLS

- Needle-nose pliers
- Round-nose pliers
- Wire cutters

TECHNIQUES

- Opening and Closing Jump Rings
- Cutting Chain
- Forming a Wrapped Loop

Level:
♦ ♦ ♦

Time:
♦ ♦ ♦ •

Silver Shine Wrap Choker

This piece is a showstopper that you can customize to suit your style. Change the way you wrap the suede cords to create a unique look every time. The chic black and silver are a perfect fit for your favorite little black dress or other evening attire.

1 *Create the first strand.* Slide the curved tube onto the 12" (31cm) 1.8mm curb chain. Use 4mm jump rings to connect each end of the chain to the top loop on each triple-loop connector.

2 *Create the second strand.* Attach a 4mm jump ring to the middle loop on each side of the connector. Use a crimp tube to connect a 16" (41cm) length of beading wire to one of those jump rings. String on an alternating pattern of 1 bicone and 1 E-bead until you have strung a total of 45 bicones and 44 E-beads. Use a crimp tube to connect the end of this wire to the 4mm jump ring on the middle loop of the other connector.

3 *Create the third strand.* Use 4mm jump rings to connect each end of the 13" (33cm) 2 x 3mm chain to the bottom loop on each connector. Use an 8mm jump ring to attach the charm to the middle of the chain.

4 *Start the choker.* Cut the suede into two 33" (84cm) lengths. Attach crimped cord ends to one end of both lengths. Use two 4mm jump rings per side to connect the cord ends to the single loop side of each connector.

5 *Continue the choker.* Cut the other end of both lengths of suede into a "v" shape. Thread the "v" through the small opening of each cone, then attach a crimped cord end to both lengths. Attach a 4mm jump ring to each cord end.

6 *Embellish one side.* Cut a 12" (31cm) length of monofilament. String on a bicone, then bring the monofilament back down through the bicone one more time to anchor it onto the bicone. Tie the monofilament into an overhand knot just below the bicone and trim the excess tail. String on an alternating pattern of 1 E-bead and 1 bicone and repeat 5 more times so that you have a total of 7 bicones and 6 E-beads on the strand. Bring the monofilament through one of the 4mm jump rings from Step 5, then back through the jump ring one more time to anchor the monofilament to the jump ring. Continue stringing on beads by repeating the beading pattern, in reverse, ending with a bicone secured the same way the other end is secured.

SHOPPING LIST

- 97 - 4mm crystal bicone beads (AB mirror blue/gray)
- 88 - 6/0 E-beads (gunmetal)
- 1 - 3mm x 50mm curved tube bead (silver)
- 1 - 16mm round charm (silver/rhinestone)
- 2 - Triple-loop connectors (silver)
- 12" (31cm) - 1.8mm curb chain (silver)
- 13" (33cm) - 2 x 3mm curb chain (silver)
- 66" (168cm) - 3mm flat suede cord (black)
- 16" (41cm) - Beading wire (silver)
- 48" (125cm) - 2 lb. monofilament (clear)
- 2 - 18 x 8mm cones (silver)
- 4 - 4mm crimped cord ends (silver)
- 2 - Crimp tubes (silver)
- 12 - 4mm jump rings (silver)
- 1 - 8mm jump ring (silver)

TOOLS

- Needle-nose pliers
- Crimping pliers
- Wire cutters
- Scissors

TECHNIQUES

- Opening and Closing Jump Rings
- Attaching Crimp Tubes/Beads
- Attaching Crimped Cord Ends
- Cutting Chain
- Simple Knots: Overhand Knot

7   *Finish one side.* Repeat Step 6, this time only stringing a total of 6 bicones and 5 E-beads on the strand. Pull the finished tassel up into the cone.

8   *Finish the choker.* Repeat Steps 6-7 on the jump ring on the other length of suede from Step 5.

Level:
◆◆◆

Time:
◆◆●

Gold Glimmer Necklace

The neutral colors of this necklace will pair well with any outfit. The bead drops and pendant tassel add a bit of movement. Create matching earrings by making six extra bead drops in Step 8 and attaching three bead drops each to a pair of earring wires.

1. *Start the pendant.* Cut an 8" (21cm) length of wire and form a briolette wire-wrapped loop at the top of the druzy pendant. Connect a 4mm jump ring to the loop.

2. *Make long bead links.* Slide 7 gold/cream bicones onto an eye pin and form a loop. Repeat to make a total of 6 long bead links.

3. *Make short bead links.* Slide a gold/cream bicone, a brass bicone, a 6mm round bead, a brass bicone, and a gold/cream bicone onto an eye pin and form a loop. Repeat to make a total of 4 short bead links.

4. *Prepare the chains.* Cut one 1½" (3.8cm) and two 3¾" (9.5cm) lengths of chain.

5. *Connect the chains and bead links.* Connect the following, in order, to the 4mm jump ring from Step 1 to form one side of the necklace: a long bead link, a 4mm jump ring, a short bead link, a 4mm jump ring, a long bead link, a 4mm jump ring, a short bead link, a 4mm jump ring, a long bead link, and a 3¾" (9.5cm) length of chain. Repeat for the other side of the necklace.

6. *Add the clasp and extender chain.* Use a 4mm jump ring to connect a lobster clasp to the end of the chain on one side of the necklace. Use a 6mm jump ring to connect the 1½" (3.8cm) length of chain to the end of the chain on the other side of the necklace. This is an extender chain.

7. *Embellish the extender chain.* Slide a gold/cream bicone and a brass bicone onto an eye pin and form a loop. Connect the brass bicone side of this bead link to the end of the extender chain. Slide a brass bicone onto a head pin and form a loop. Connect this bead drop to the other end of the bead link.

8. *Make the bead drops.* Slide a bronze bicone, a gold/cream bicone, and a bronze bicone onto a head pin and form a loop. Repeat to make a total of 10 small bead drops.

SHOPPING LIST

- 1 - 27 x 20mm natural druzy crystal pendant (white)
- 5 - 6mm round beads (AB mirror gold/cream)
- 61 - 4mm glass bicone beads (AB mirror gold/cream)
- 32 - 4mm glass bicone beads (AB mirror brass)
- 16" (41cm) - 4mm flat-link cable chain (antique gold)
- 8" (21cm) - 24-gauge wire (gold)
- 11 - 2" (5cm) eye pins (antique gold)
- 12 - 1" (2.5cm) head pins (antique gold)
- 11 - 4mm jump rings (antique gold)
- 1 - 6mm jump ring (antique gold)
- 1 - Lobster clasp (antique gold)

TOOLS

- Needle-nose pliers
- Round-nose pliers
- Wire cutters

TECHNIQUES

- Opening and Closing Jump Rings
- Cutting Chain
- Forming a Loop
- Forming a Loop for Briolette Beads

9   *Add the bead drops.* Connect 1 small bead drop from Step 8 to each side of the 4mm jump ring connected to the wrapped loop on top of the druzy pendant. Connect 1 small bead drop to the outside edge of each of the 4mm jump rings linking the long and short bead links together on each side of the necklace.

10   *Embellish the pendant.* Cut one 3-link and two 8-link lengths of chain. Slide one end of each length of chain onto a 4mm jump ring. Put the jump ring around the base of the wire wrapped loop on top of the druzy pendant so that the chains hang down over the front of the pendant.

11   *Finish embellishing the pendant.* Slide a brass bicone, a 6mm round bead, and a brass bicone onto a head pin and form a loop. Connect this bead drop to the other end of the 3-link length of chain from Step 10.

Green Goddess Headpiece

Embrace your inner earth goddess and rock this cool headpiece. The design is light, simple, and easy to wear and is sure to be a conversation piece. Complete this look with an earthy palette of browns, greens, and creams and accents made of natural materials like leather and rope.

1 *Cut the chain.* Cut the following lengths of chain: one 22" (56cm), one 10½" (27cm), two 5¾" (14.5cm), and one 4" (10.5cm).

2 *Make the bead drops.* Slide the green teardrop onto a head pin and form a loop to make a teardrop bead drop. Slide the green bicone onto a head pin and form a loop to make a bicone bead drop.

3 *Attach the first chain.* Using 4mm jump rings, attach the 22" (56cm) chain to each end loop on the bottom of the connector. This section of chain lies around the head, above the ears.

4 *Attach the second chain.* Use 4mm jump rings to attach one end of the 10½" (27cm) chain to the large open top loop of the connector and the other end to the center link of the 22" (56cm) chain. This section of chain lies on top of the head, front to back.

5 *Attach the third chain.* Use 4mm jump rings to connect one end of the 4" (10.5cm) chain to each of the second loops on the bottom of the connector.

6 *Attach the final chains.* Attach one end of the 5¾" (14.5cm) chains to each of the jump rings used in Step 5. Attach the other ends of the 5¾" (14.5cm) chains to the 22" (56cm) chain, about 2¾" (7cm) out from the connector.

7 *Add the rear embellishment.* Use a 4mm jump ring to connect the teardrop bead drop to the bottom center loop of the connector. Use a 6mm jump ring to connect the charm to the bottom of the small top loop of the connector, so that the charm hangs down into the middle of the large bottom loop of the connector.

8 *Add the front embellishment.* Attach the bicone bead drop to the bottom of the center link of the 22" (56cm) chain, so that the drop hangs down in the middle of the forehead.

SHOPPING LIST

- 1 - 6mm charm (antique gold/green)
- 1 - 10 x 5mm crystal teardrop (green)
- 1 - 6mm crystal bicone (green)
- 1 - 34 x 20mm chandelier loop connector (antique gold)
- 50" (130cm) - 4mm flat-link cable chain (antique gold)
- 2 - 1" (2.5cm) head pins (antique gold)
- 9 - 4mm jump rings (antique gold)
- 1 - 6mm jump ring (antique gold)

TOOLS

- Needle-nose pliers
- Round-nose pliers
- Wire cutters

TECHNIQUES

- Opening and Closing Jump Rings
- Cutting Chain
- Forming a Loop

Tip: Adjust the chain lengths used in Step 3 (22" [56cm]) and Step 4 (10½" [27cm]) as needed for different head sizes.

Boho Stone Drop Necklace

Level:
♦ ♦ ♦

Time:
♦ ● ●

This necklace has a funky tribal look that will be a perfect fit for your summer wardrobe. Pair it with a tank top, shorts, and your favorite flips-flops. Change up the pattern or the color of the bead drops to match your personal style.

1 *Make the first bead drop.* Cut a 10" (25.5cm) length of wire. Center an orange dagger bead on the wire. Thread each end of the wire through the corresponding holes in a small orange pyramid and then a large orange pyramid. Thread both wire ends through an orange nugget. Form a wrapped loop at the top of the nugget bead that is large enough for the tan suede cord to pass through.

2 *Make the remaining bead drops.* Repeat Step 1 with the remaining beads in each color to create 10 bead drops total, 2 in each color.

3 *Attach the first bead drop.* Cut a 28" (72cm) length of tan suede cord. String an orange bead drop onto the cord and position it about 7¾" (19.7cm) from one end of the cord. Tie an overhand knot in the cord around the loop of the bead drop to secure it in place.

4 *Attach the remaining bead drops.* Repeat Step 3 with a green bead drop, positioning it about ½" (1.3cm) from the orange bead drop. Continue repeating this step to add the remaining bead drops, spaced about ½" (1.3cm) apart, in the following order: yellow, blue, purple, orange, green, yellow, blue, purple.

5 *Attach the paper cord.* Cut a 28" (72cm) length of brown paper cord. Match one end of the paper cord with the end of the suede cord that is 7¾" (19.7cm) from the first bead drop. Secure both cords in a crimped cord end.

6 *Wrap the bead drops.* Bring the brown cord down along the suede cord. At each bead drop, wrap the brown cord once tightly around the top of each bead drop and continue on.

7 *Finish the necklace.* Bring the brown cord up along the suede cord on the other side of the necklace. Trim both cords to 7¾" (19.7cm) past the last bead drop. Secure both cords in a crimped cord end.

8 *Attach the clasp.* Attach a 6mm jump ring to each crimped cord end. Attach the lobster clasp to one of the jump rings.

SHOPPING LIST

- 2 of each color - 6mm 2-hole pyramid glass beads (orange, green, yellow, blue, purple)
- 2 of each color - 12mm 2-hole pyramid glass beads (orange, green, yellow, blue, purple)
- 2 of each color - 3 x 11mm dagger drop glass beads (orange, green, yellow, blue, purple)
- 2 of each color - 10mm nugget glass beads (orange, green, yellow, blue, purple)
- 9' (275cm) - 24-gauge wire (gold)
- 28" (72cm) - 3mm suede cord (tan)
- 28" (72cm) - 1.5mm paper cord (brown)
- 2 - 4mm crimped cord ends (gold)
- 2 - 6mm jump rings (gold)
- 1 - Lobster clasp (gold)

TOOLS

- Needle-nose pliers
- Round-nose pliers
- Wire cutters
- Scissors

TECHNIQUES

- Opening and Closing Jump Rings
- Attaching Crimped Cord Ends
- Forming a Wrapped Loop
- Simple Knots: Overhand Knot

GLOSSARY

Here are a few more miscellaneous terms you might encounter in the Shopping Lists in this book and in the jewelry aisles at your local craft store. For the definitions of most other tools and materials mentioned in this book, see pages 8–11.

Miscellaneous Terms

AB: standing for "aurora borealis," a type of bead finish applied to one side of the bead that reflects different iridescent colors.

druzy crystal: a stone with many tiny, fine crystals on top of a colorful mineral. They are very sparkly and colorful.

extender chain: a short length of chain used at the clasp to make the size of a jewelry piece flexible.

lariat: a necklace style that has a long, straight drop coming from the middle of the necklace. This type of necklace usually does not have a clasp.

Key Types of Chain

cable chain: chain that has interlocking links that are either round or oval in shape.

curb chain: chain that has interlocking links that are semi-curved and seem to interlock on an angle, allowing the chain to lie flat.

flat-link chain: any chain that has interlocking links where each link is somewhat flattened on its sides.

double-link chain: any chain that has two links paired up in place of single links.

drawn cable chain: cable chain with links that are stretched/elongated.

rope chain: chain that has multiple layers of links connected in a spiral-esque pattern, creating a rope effect.

figure-8 chain: chain that has figure-8 shaped links.

Features of Key Materials for Beads/Pendants

glass: very widely available, cheap to expensive, many different cuts and shapes.

crystal: widely available, cheap to expensive.

acrylic: widely available, affordable.

resin: less widely available, affordable.

gemstone: widely available, affordable to expensive, heavy weight.

INDEX